# THE WISDOM
## OF THE
# GUARDIAN

[The Best of the Guardian Code]

## STEVE SHENK

PUBLISHED BY FIDELI PUBLISHING INC.

Copyright © 2013 by Steven Shenk.

All rights reserved.

Except as permitted under the U.S. Copyright Act of 1976, no part of this publication may be reproduced, distributed, or transmitted in any form or by any means or stored in a database or retrieval system, without the prior written permission of the publisher.

ISBN#: 978-1-60414-728-5

Originally Published by Grape Vine Blue, LLC, 2012.

Visit our Websites:

**www.SteveShenk.com**

**www.TheGuardianCode.com**

First Edition: January 2013.
Second Edition. October 2013

Cover Design by Fideli Publishing

COMPANION BOOKS:

*The Guardian Code*

*My Book of Life*

PRINTED IN THE UNITED STATES OF AMERICA

# Food for Thought...

Our progress in life is like climbing a ladder. Until you have climbed onto the first rung you have no chance of getting to the second rung or the third rung on up to the top. A baby is born and the first and only concern he has is for food—the FIRST RUNG ON THE LADDER OF LIFE. Everything that crosses his path goes into the mouth and there ain't going to be no further progression until that "job one" gets done.

So...what's the difference between this baby, an executive in too much debt, a homeless person, and a recent victim of a natural disaster?

Absolutely none! Every one of these individuals has been dropped back down life's ladder to the most basic bottom rung: the necessity for sustenance or FOOD.

We as human beings have four aspects to our total makeup. We are physical, mental, emotional, and spiritual beings.

As we climb the ladder of our life's progression, each of the steps prepares us and allows us to climb to the next rung. Until we have filled our need for food and other physical necessities, we can't climb to the thinking (or mental) rung on our ladder, much less move upward to the emotional and spiritual aspects of our life's progressions.

Perfect examples are slavery, sharecropping, feudalism, and totalitarian regimes. The majority of people are kept at the most basic level of survival, spending every waking hour focused on just providing food for themselves. They are never allowed to progress to the thinking (or mental) step on their ladder of progression. If this were allowed they would very shortly progress to the emotional level which would cause the motivation to rebel for independence.

It's interesting to note that the thousands of families that I've worked with over the years have been working for preparedness. They realized that food is every human being's greatest concern in the face of adversity or crisis.

What these prudent individuals understood is that no matter what their present circumstances—rich or poor, secure or insecure—when hard times hit, every one of us is thrown back to the bottom of the ladder where the first thing we must provide is food.

They say that he who does not learn from history is destined to repeat it. History has shown us that no matter what your belief, what your circumstance, where you live, or who you are, one way or another, good times will always be followed by bad times… and bad times, fortunately, will always be followed by good times.

We come back full circle to the question of why on earth would a food guy write a book on life, about the laws that create joy, peace, happiness, and the magnificence of a human life? It's very simple. I spent three decades helping thousands of people climb the first rung of he four-step ladder of becoming who they can be. In providing food for the physical aspect of their beings I have learned that the mental, emotional, and spiritual aspects of people also need "comfort food-for-thought" of the knowledge that they can be masters of their destinies and captains of their souls.

In these troubled times of worldwide famine, when half the population of our country needs assistance with their food budgets, when millions of American children don't have food, when millions of us are without employment, when millions have lost their homes, when depression is a major illness, when stress (a form of fear) contributes to the five major killer diseases of our people, when the majority of us feel like victims, I ask: WHAT DO YOU WANT ME TO DO?

If I have learned the universal and eternal laws by which you can take back your liberty, your freedom, and your independence, would you not want me to tell you?

Would those of you who don't have enough food to eat or a home to live in want to know the laws and principles that you have within your power to provide for your needs?

The extent to which any of us is dependent is the extent to which we have given power over ourselves to that on which we depend. Would any of you who hope that you have magnificence built into your very being not want to know how to reach out and grab independence by the throat and hang on for dear life?

No, my beloved friends, having learned these principles and being made aware of these laws that are expressed by The Guardian in this book, it would be the most despicable of crimes on my part if I did not share them as powerfully as I can. The objective is to enable every soul—every soul who chooses to be a student to whom the teacher must appear—to learn and use them, reaching the magnificence in the measure of their creation.

To this end I commit all of the power of my being that you might live long and prosper with dignity, joy, and peace of mind. It is my wish that one day, in the not-too-distant future, you and I can smile when we say to each other "I like me best when I'm with you."

That's why I believe The Wisdom of the Guardian is something we all experience, and that we can all share with one another…on a daily basis. Something to chew on…

*~ Steve Shenk*

# Introduction

Actually, you are partly responsible for our putting this small book of quotes together. So, here it is… mainly because you asked for it.

When we began setting down the chapters and notes from the first draft of *THE GUARDIAN CODE: It's Not Your Fault [And I Can Prove It!]*, we found that the Guardian had so much to say that we couldn't let it go to waste. So we peppered each chapter with his favorite quips, quotable quotes and personal tips until they almost formed a bunch of chapters in and of themselves. (In fact, they do, in exact reference, chronological order and replication of the original book—virtually chapter and verse—the best of the best.)

Pithy, poignant and to the point, *The Wisdom of the Guardian* is carefully crafted out of direct quotes from The Guardian presented to you in simple, direct, and memorable ways that anyone can grasp…and share!

So, it has become the ultimate reference point to help you introduce your friends and people you care about to the secrets of *THE GUARDIAN CODE: It's Not Your Fault [And I Can Prove It!]*.

Nothing does a better job in a shorter time than being able to tap into The Guardian Code itself—how daily application of these quotes help to tie everything together—and how it will help create a quick and powerful reference point that is as close as your purse or pocket.

And you can even quote yourself and share your own thoughts. If there's anything The Guardian Code will teach you it's that you too have something worth saying. As such you are truly being taught to become your own guru, sage, teacher and mystical counselor. So, we have a "NOTES" section at the end of this for you to write down your own thoughts.

Everything wise that we do in life comes from the same Source. So, when an interesting idea occurs to you—whether it is something you found on these pages, somewhere else, or just came up with yourself, write it down…and put it out there! That's how people grow. That's when you come to realize that truly, "It's Not Your Fault."

In fact, it's your Opportunity…to share and expand the experience.

## PROLOGUE

# A Personal Note from The Guardian

*Taking guiltless—faultless—responsibility for your controllable interest in any situation will resolve all problems and fill your life with peace, joy, freedom, and happiness. Think about it.*

*— The Guardian*

# 1

# Michael Meets the Guardian

*These simple principles are not new. They're proven successful, because they are the application of eternal universal laws. Great masters, prophets, teachers, and messengers have been sent to mankind at various intervals throughout the turbulent history of this tiny planet. Their job has been to share these universal laws with humankind and to their discovery to help guide them out of the darkness. (The problem has come in the translation.)*

# 2

# People Think Life Has Handed them a Lemon

*What evil men do is what we see. The good is not newsworthy. Think about it.*

# 3

# Your Life Is Like a Perfect Building

*When there is no justification for Guilt, does that mean that the individual is innocent? What is the adjective we most often use to describe a newborn baby? Innocent! What is a life that is Innocent? Is it Perfect? If there was a mechanism in a human life that was able to remove Guilt, could that life not remain perfect? Think about it.*

---

*There was a poster on the wall of an orphanage in New York. It was a picture of a scruffy, ragged little girl. The caption under the picture said, "I know I'm somebody because God don't make no trash." Think about it!*

---

*People remain perfect all of their lives, while they train themselves for the potential they've chosen to obtain. Try though we have, over the centuries, no mortal has yet proven the optimum potential that a complex spiritual, emotional, intelligent physical human being can achieve. Think about it!*

# 4

# The Magic of Faultlessness

*Remember, no one ever intentionally does anything stupid. Think about it.*

———

*If two people see the same information from the same perspective with the same objective, their decisions won't be defective. There'll be no illusion about their conclusion. Think about it.*

———

*Miracles will happen if every confrontation is begun with the statement, "It's Not Your Fault, and I can prove it." It's also not my fault, and I can prove that too. Finding Fault solves nothing. Taking responsibility solves everything. Think about it.*

# 5

# Guilt: The "UnOriginal" Sin

*Guilt is often the basis of many religions when that was anything but the teaching of their founders. In Christianity, the concept of Original Sin (having to do with carnal knowledge and the fall from Eden) took hold in the Fourth Century A.D., and seemed designed to condemn the innocent child—virtually out of the womb—to a life of imperfection, moral depravity, and Guilt. Some may call it Sin, but sin by any other name has the same root cause—Guilt.*

*Traditionally, priests, ministers, bishops, cardinals, and medicine men were all dispensers of Guilt. It came through Judgment and was often corrected through something called 'penance' and a forgiveness of sins. In the Middle Ages, that forgiveness could actually be purchased (in the same way you'd pay a traffic ticket), and those purchases actually had a name—Indulgences. Most of the time, indulgences were only available to those who could afford them. So people came to believe that there was literally a price to be paid for redemption. At the same time, they looked upon this concept as corrupt and the very notion of "forgiveness" to be flawed, especially since it seemed more available to those with enough money to actually pay for it. In a way, even in our modern Republic, people still believe that there are two kinds of justice— one for the rich and one for the rest of us.*

*So people are less and less inclined to think that we have a level playing field. And nothing is more of a seedbed for guilt and victimization than that. Think about it.*

---

*Racism, prejudice, and bigotry are the result of judging others who look or believe differently than we do and pre-assuming on their behalf a challenge to our own beliefs. (I need everybody to be just like me, because if they aren't the question is raised in my own mind as to whether I am right.) Often adherents to a belief system will proselytize desperately to "save from hell and misery" the object of their attention when their true underlying need is to justify their own uncertain convictions. (This is a common application of the Horse Manure Principal, which states, "Eat horse manure. One hundred and fifty billion flies can't be wrong.") Think about it.*

---

*That which I find in you that offends me, I have in me, for if I did not have it in me I could not see it in you. Students will note that the lack of Judgmentalism on the part of a Master, Sensei, or great teacher is the result of the attribute of guiltlessness. Think about it.*

---

*Don't forget the universal law that states: "No one ever does anything intentionally stupid." This doesn't necessarily mean that what was done was either correct or appropriate. That is why understanding the Guilt Trash Removal System is so valuable. Think about it.*

---

*More and more people are actually beginning to acknowledge the validity of the 'It's Not Your Fault,' concept. A recent cartoon in The New Yorker showed a family of four lost deep in the African jungle. In it, the father is addressing his wife and children with this ironic caption: 'Okay, I acknowledge that we're lost. The important thing is to stay focused on whose fault it is.' Funny stuff, when you think about it.*

---

*The things about you that offend me are qualities I actually have myself, for if I did not have them in me I could not recognize them in you. One of the greatest things that can be said about any human being is that they are 'guileless.' Look at the spelling of the word, 'guile,' and the word 'guilt' and tell me the linguistic root of these words. Is it reasonable to assume that the truly guileless person is devoid of personal guilt and thus sees nothing objectionable in others? Think about it.*

## 6

# Victims Have Big 'Buts'

*There are four easy ways to spot a Victim. And once you get the hang of it, Victims are easy to spot. 1) Victims always spend their last dime before they make arrangements to get the next one. People who are in control of their lives don't spend their last dime until they have their fist around their next one. 2) Victims lose things all the time—more often than not, they're 'stolen.' Positive people are well organized, seldom lose things, and always seem to be in the right place at the right time. 3) Victims always seem to be equally creative at being in the wrong place at precisely the right time, and are always convinced that Murphy's Law applies to them more than anyone else. They lose their money. Their purse was stolen. The car they bought is a lemon. Their appearance is sloppy. Their grammar is poor. And they're always rationalizing the reasons that everything happens to them. 4) Victims are never in control of their lives. People in control of their lives are always the ones you admire. They seem to have their act together. And other people want to be around them. They're always the ones victims see as 'lucky.' They're the ones who get all the breaks, while the victims never have any. Think about it.*

# 7

# You Say You Love Me. Prove It!

*The behaviors exhibited by Enablees to control and manipulate their Enablers are the same as those used by terrorists against their victims. (Enablees are, however, often less covert.) Think about it.*

———

*Look at the track record of Israeli terrorist response teams. The Israelis have an absolute carved-in-granite policy never to negotiate with terrorists. They completely ignore the 'care enough' blackmail model to do what the terrorists insist is the 'right course of action.' The Israeli response to this is: 'Do what you've got to do. But we refuse to recognize any hold you think you may have over us.' The result is that terrorists, who have been known to hold out for days, either abandon their position or surrender within minutes of being notified that an Israeli anti-terrorist team is on the scene. Think about it.*

## 8

# The Past Does Not Exist

*If you have truly repented (and that means you are not recreating the event in your mind over and over and over again), the past is gone. At the point where you have asked for forgiveness, at the point where you've made restitution and at the point where you've decided you don't ever want it to happen again, it's done—unless, of course, you go back and relive it over and over again, which might be looked upon as committing the sin again.*

*Think about it.*

———

*When the fire was destroying his buildings, rather than commiserating over the disaster, he is said to have called for others to come and enjoy the spectacular event with him. Thomas Edison lived to be 85 years old, continuing to invent and build until the week he died. Thomas Edison—the holder of more than 1,500 patents and the inventor of everything from control of electric current to the motion picture camera—never dwelled in the past and never concerned himself with the future. By his own self-description, he lived and thrived in The Now, and understood better than anyone that this moment is all that matters. Think about it.*

———

*No thing, no one, and no experience can have an impact on your life unless you allow it to. Those who live in the past, those who obsess over it, those who allow any experience from the past to affect them other than their choice to learn from history, are fools, and they only victimize themselves. No ifs, ands, or BUTS about it. Think about it.*

## 9

# The Law of Me

*A most important law that we all must remember is that when someone acts or speaks in a negative way toward us it is never about us, it is always about them. Believe it. It is always about them. Think about it.*

---

*In a romantic relationship or a marriage, the difference between making love and having sex lies in the physical expression of it. Making love is the physical expression of no-fault, no-judgment unconditional acceptance of one person by another. Having sex is the seeking of counterfeit approval and never finding it. One is spiritual and clear; the other is both polluted and superficial. Tell me, Michael, would you rather be with a woman who judges, evaluates and rewards you with her 'approval' based on the orgasmic output you elicit in her? Or would you rather be with a woman who savors a touch or a hug from you as readily as she enjoys complete physical intimacy? A truly loved woman can release the troubles of the world as easily by holding hands on a quiet walk as she can from the ecstasy of a nude embrace. So the choice is yours. Which would you rather have: unconditional (it's not your fault) appreciation and acceptance? Or the judgmental hoops and traps of reward and punishment, endlessly searching yet never finding the peace of being able to say, 'I like me best when I'm with you? Think about it.*

---

*On an individual scale, fault-finding as it applies to the Law of Me is both sad and self-destructive. On a global scale, it can be dangerous and occasionally even disastrous. There are records upon records to show that many international calamities such as airplane crashes, the Titanic, even Pearl Harbor, all quite probably took place because people concealed, delayed, or ignored critical information for fear of being found at fault. In other words, they were afraid to take responsibility for their actions. Think about it.*

———

*If you have ever been to a Little League baseball game you will often see fathers, who were never good ballplayers themselves, pushing hard for the achievements of their children in order to vicariously experience the success they were never able to achieve themselves. Think about it.*

———

*How does the inflated ego of the alms giver affect the self-image of the recipient of their alms? Think about it.*

## 10

# Self-Image: The Great Mirror

*"Who am I? Am I who I think I am or am I who you think I am or am I who I think you think I am?" This is a conversation everyone has with himself, whether he (or she) does so consciously, or not. Think about it.*

---

*The 'mirror technique' of telling yourself who you will become and what you will achieve is a valuable application of the personal Law of Creation. This technique is extremely effective. Many entertainers and public personalities have used it successfully. As an example, it has been said that Barbra Streisand adopted this very method to train herself to sing so beautifully. Think about it.*

---

*Minorities in any situation, rather than kick against the pricks of resistance and demand to be accepted, would be very wise to find the things that appeal to the other races and play them like a fiddle. Out-dress them, outsmart them, out-talk them—not in a malicious way, but because that's just how things are. Think about it.*

*If you want to be good at a sport, separate yourself and get rid of the negative feedback that tears down your self-image. That way your image of yourself is what you will do with what you project onto the Screen of Life. By being by yourself, you don't have to be thinking, "Who is watching and what do they think?" with every move you make. That way—when preparing, when practicing, when in the middle of a game—you can perform only the 'good stuff.' And that becomes your Self-image. Think about it.*

———

*People with low self-esteem very often try to use financial leverage to create images of themselves that will broadcast their worth to everyone else. They may not be personally attractive, but they can adjust the image they project to others by the house they own, the car they drive, the clubs they belong to, the trophy wife, and the other 'cool possessions' that they have. In doing so, they are creating status-symbol billboards about who they are in hopes of convincing everyone else that they are who they seem to be. Ultimately, they only attract others who are projecting the same illusions of status. Think about it.*

———

*This concept is not as complicated as it seems. And it might be better expressed in a popular anecdote about world famous actor/ comedian Groucho Marx. Groucho (who had very few problems with self-esteem) tried for years to get into the Los Angeles Country Club, a notoriously snooty golf club that had restrictions against admitting both Jews and actors for membership. Even though Groucho was very well connected, he was both an actor and a Jew. So his appeals to join were rejected for over 10 years. Finally, with some considerable leverage exercised on his behalf by board members, Groucho received a letter of acceptance from LA Country Club and immediately fired back his reply: 'I'm sorry. But after careful consideration, I've decided I don't want to belong to any club that wants me for a member.' Think about it.*

---

*People can actually destroy themselves by their own Self-Image. By the insertion of Guilt into the equation of who they are, they can actually 'de-perfectize' themselves, as it were (creating a lack of perfection). The child, who starts out in life as perfect, goes out and does something he has been trained not to do, and becomes disappointed in himself; so he quickly starts to see himself as something that is less than perfect. So these people become disappointed in themselves; their mask of 'perfection' has been stripped away from them, and they're no longer who they seem to be. (After all, you can't fool yourself.) Suddenly everything they do is an expression of their imperfection. They take on more bad habits. They get bad grades. They let their good credit slide by not paying bills. 'What the hell, let it all go down!' (Their perfection has been marred to begin with, and anything that mars their perfection destroys them.) They feel boxed-in. They feel that it's all their fault, and they can never get back to their perfect state. The whole idea behind knowing 'It's Not Your Fault' is finding a way to break out of that box. Perfection has not been destroyed beyond repair. You can get back to perfection. And it starts here: This is the repair process. Think about it.*

## 11

# Judgment

*It is of interest to note that the statue representing justice standing on the steps of our courthouses holds in her hand a balanced scale and wears a blindfold. Think about it.*

———

*It has been said that, 'The Dog is Man's Best Friend.' Isn't it a pity that man can't be man's best friend? But do you know what the difference is? Human beings hold the issue of Judgment as an asset when it is, in fact, their greatest liability—and they use it to limit both their humanity and their human potential to achieve great things. Dogs can be man's best friends because they simply have no comprehension of how to be judgmental. You'd have to walk a very long way to find a judgmental, arrogant, gossiping, egotistical, self-righteous, and righteously indignant puppy. Think about it.*

———

*Applications of Justice in our everyday lives take place at the most elementary levels of consciousness (some of them even cellular). In so-called 'primitive societies,' the harvesting of plant life is undertaken with an eye toward conserving the life of the very plant from which the harvest is taken. (Only a portion of the plant is removed. This way it is allowed to renew itself.) What's more, a verbal thanksgiving is extended in gratitude to that plant for providing the gift of life…In the same societies the same rules are applied to the hunting and 'harvesting' of animals. And as they take the life of the animal that is to become their food, they offer their prayers of thanksgiving to this other intelligence that has offered itself so that they might continue to live another day.*

*To understand this kind of 'cellular application of the law' we point to a couple of experiments performed by Cleve Backster at the Institute of Transpersonal Psychology in Palo Alto, California. A former consultant with the CIA, Backster applied a polygraph machine to two sets of plants to confirm earlier findings that plants are sentient—that they experience emotions such as pain, pleasure, fear, and affection, and that they have the ability to communicate with humans and other forms of life in a recognizable manner.*

*To reinforce this, Chinese Capsicum plants were divided into two groups—Group One had sensors attached to their leaves and Group Two was left in pots with no sensors. At that point two students were selected—one Abuser, one Caregiver. The Abuser would come into the room, go to the unmonitored plants and abuse them verbally, physically, and any other way they could think of (stopping just short of destroying them entirely). Later, a Caregiver would enter, going to the same plants to extend them every courtesy—nurturing, touching them lovingly and even playing them selections of classical music. After several cycles in this pattern, the 'terrorist' student would enter the room and the polygraph-monitored plants would register high levels of pain and panic, virtually screaming at this person's presence. Conversely, when the caregiver student came back into the room, the plants with sensor monitors would respond with peaceful, calm, low-stress measurements, often calming to lower than normal registrations on the meter.*

*In other words, the plants responded at very profound ranges of cellular sensitivity to both extreme levels of abuse and tender loving care shown to them. Think about it.*

## 12

# Approval

*Much human activity of a spiritual nature—whether it's expressed in primitive tribes to 'appease the Gods' or in modern religious rules that require us to 'act correctly' or seek the forgiveness and approval of God through prayer and fasting—is more often than not inconsistent with the "unconditional" definition of God-like love. So, seeking Approval (Unconditional Love) of a disapproving God automatically becomes an oxymoron. Think about it.*

―――

*Even if physical force is applied, an often quoted rhyme, 'The mind that's changed against its will is of the same opinion still,' is still the way things work. Think about it.*

―――

*There's an interesting aspect to enthusiastically showing approval. It's a release. But it can also be artificial. Think about the last time you attended a motivational seminar. At the end there's a great deal of applause—maybe even a standing ovation. And some of the applause is for yourself because it's kind of a feel-good feedback you get for having attended the event. But very often applause diffuses the true emotion. What if somebody stuffed that enthusiasm, and actually decided instead to go out and act upon the information they just received? It's a fact that people forget*

90 percent of what they hear and see at motivational events within 24 hours. What if they just sat and mentally absorbed what they had just learned. How much more of it would they actually retain? Think about it.

---

In reality, most great achievements are the result of the "achiever" stretching his or her skills "outside the box" of conventional thinking (Approval) and being confident in their own Approval of their creativity. Think about it.

---

Unfortunately, putting "conditions" on love and approval is so much the rule rather than the exception that very few children have the tremendous advantage of experiencing an early life free of Conditional Love and the manipulation that comes with it. Think about it.

---

Here's a test for the next time you get aggravated with having to change a diaper. If you've read this section and understand how these principles really work, you're obligated to immediately make up a sign—no matter how silly you think it is—that says: It's Not Your Fault, and put it up over your baby's crib. If you get that, you've made it nicely to this point. If you don't, you won't be able to comprehend one more word in this book. (So don't mess with me. Just do what you're told.) Think about it.

---

*Physical contact is extremely important to human beings. There is an old saying that everyone needs at least eight hugs a day. A study with troubled youth indicates that light stroking on the back and touching or a hug with positive brief conversation at bedtime is very calming and establishes a strong, bonded working relationship. Think about it.*

---

*There are times when individuals intentionally choose to be mean and behave badly toward you. If there is no misunderstanding for you to clarify it is important for you to understand that their behavior and attitude is never about you and always about them. It would then be wise to remove yourself from the relationship since it would be inappropriate to infringe on their intentional choices. (The Native Americans have an interesting philosophy with regard to impossible situations. They say, 'When the horse being ridden dies the wise man dismounts.') Think about it.*

## 13

# Unconditional Love

*The reactions we have to other people are judgments that we feel they are causing us to make of ourselves. If you will recall, anger and judgmentalism are both evidence of underlying Guilt. Think about it.*

―――

*With all this in mind, it is important—in the quest for this state—to set the right kind of goals. As is the case with all goals, we have to ask the questions: What is it you want? Why do you want that? Is wealth a means in itself? Or is it just a means of getting something else—perhaps to accomplish something better? The key is an element called Desire, because desire can also cross over into a sense of lack. So you have to ask yourself what the true purpose is for your goals. Once you've done that, release all thoughts and feelings that would limit you: the ones that say, 'you can't have it.' If your goal is abundance, visualize that there are no limits to your abundance. By removing limits, we are able to focus on intention and our subconscious is free to fly to places our conscious mind cannot even comprehend. Do this often enough, and you can master the physical world. So, creating abundance becomes an effortless act. Think about it.*

## 14

# Agency:
# The Freedom to Choose

*In making choices it is wise to consider, 'whether the view is worth the effort of the climb.' Think about it.*

---

*A unique concept in choices and decision-making known only to Guardians is use of the question: Can you afford to be wrong? A simple example: You are attending an outdoor event. The weather looks like it could be rainy. To carry an umbrella would be a nuisance if you didn't need it. Ask the question "With which choice can I afford to be wrong? If I take the umbrella and there's no rain, I'm wrong, but no problem. If I don't take the umbrella, and it rains, I'm wrong and miserable. So, your decision becomes evident: Take the umbrella. With that choice you can afford to be wrong. Think about it.*

---

*Remember the thought that, 'A mind that's changed against its will is of the same opinion still.' Think about it.*

---

*It is common for people to challenge the idea that nothing can affect them except as they choose to allow it. It is true that someone can punch you in the mouth. Lies can be told about you. You can be placed in prison. Your stuff can be stolen. Your love can be betrayed. Your needs can be denied. BUT you and you alone choose how you allow anything, anyone or any situation to affect you. Think about it.*

## 15

# The Wonder Hugger

*The Distance Is Disaster principle is the reason that the technologically advanced communication forms of e-mails and texting are more devastating to human relationships and negotiations than folks really imagine. The words we use are only a small percentage of our total communication, lagging far behind facial, voice intonation, and body language. (This is why important negotiations must always be done face-to-face.) As a result, true communication is significantly more emotional than logical. It is frustrating to many folks that someone who wishes to avoid TRUE communication will send e-mails and texts. This practice is often construed to be and often is sneaky and disingenuous. Think about it.*

---

*You will often find that, in a heated discussion with another person, they will seemingly have a tendency to not be able to stay on the subject and follow the logic of your arguments. When this occurs they possibly might not be the sharpest tool in the shed, a dim bulb as it were. Nevertheless, in reality they are often feeling Guilt and trying to slip away from the sensitive subject, so they can direct focus away from their discomfort. Guilt can often readily be identified by the misdirection of focus from the path of logical reason. Think about it.*

---

*By becoming a Wonder Hugger instead of forcing Jim to move away from her, Sandy actually enhanced his Agency and made a deposit in his Liberty account, by giving him the freedom to choose another solution to the problem. Instead of growing increasingly angry and trying to avoid blame, he could now offer her a Wonder Hug in return. She had proved to Jim that it wasn't his fault. (It wasn't anyone's fault!) So, Jim no longer felt the need to blame her for trying to limit his choices. Think about it.*

———

*Living a no-fault life brings tremendous peace of mind. Giving no fault to another is the greatest gift of all. Think about it.*

## 16

# The Big Push...Away!

*Remember that the significance of the Law of Me is that everything a person does is based on how he wishes to be perceived by himself and others. Notice in that statement that the first and most important perception is of himself. If a person doesn't like himself and sees himself as the Victim of life with no control and no Hope, he can't possibly perceive anyone else liking him and will 'Push Away' to avoid the pain and chance of being reminded of his 'unworthiness.' Think about it.*

---

*There are a lot of good counselors and therapists that are very well meaning and help large numbers of people work through problems in their lives by rummaging around in those experiences and helping them 'relive the trauma' in order to relieve themselves of any Guilt in the experience. Human beings are peculiar in that way: anything that causes them pain is immediately evaluated in terms of whether or not it makes them feel as if they 'deserve what happened to them,' and that it may be part of the life plan they have drawn up for themselves. This kind of treatment very often stems from the fact that, consciously or subconsciously, people know that they are truly in control of their own life, and at some point they will have to take responsibility for it. Think about it.*

---

*One of the most classic cases of The Big Push (Away) comes with an entire movie devoted to the subject:* Good Will Hunting. *In the Oscar-winning film, Will, played by actor/co-writer Matt Damon, is a self-educated genius and math prodigy from the streets of South Boston who has just solved one of the most difficult mathematic equations in the history of MIT and yet is a barroom brawler on the verge of being sentenced to prison for his fifth count of simple assault. Instead, Hunting is bailed out by a Fields Medal-winning professor Gerald Lambeau (played by Stellan Skarsgård) with the stipulation that he send the young man to 'counseling'. As ordered by the court, Lambeau runs Will through a gauntlet of a dozen therapists to deal with his childhood issues of abandonment, life in an orphanage, and extreme physical abuse in a series of foster homes.*

*After each of his counselors, trying to poke around in Hunting's past, is made a fool of by his brilliant manipulations, Will is sent as a last resort to Lambeau's old college roommate Sean McGuire, played by Robin Williams. McGuire turns out to be as canny, clever, and unorthodox as Hunting is a genius at evasion. And he immediately sees Will Hunting for what he is: A master of repelling everything of value in his life—a loving girlfriend, a six-figure income, and international academic acclaim and recognition (for which he truly longs). After nearly failing himself, McGuire realizes that no conventional therapy will ever work on this unassailable genius. By now, having won Hunting's confidence by refusing to take on any Guilt, projected or otherwise, McGuire simply stands at the threshold of every dark door the young man opens inside himself and tells him: It's Not Your Fault. The phrase, repeated over and over, becomes more powerful every time it's spoken, until Will Hunting finally breaks down (and breaks through)! And yes! The scene ends in a Wonder Hug. Most healing begins and ends that way. Think about it.*

## 17

# Move Over, Casanova and Don Juan. Here comes Bob!

*The closeness and time spent with fellow employees in the workplace along with the commensurate distances from family members readily proves absolutely the universal law which states 'To Know Me Is to Love Me'. 'Bonding' will inevitably occur when people share an enhanced understanding (knowledge) of each other. Think about it.*

## 18

# I Like Me Best When I'm With You

*Love others as they deserve to be loved, since you know that it's not their fault. Think about it.*

---

*It's easy to learn what makes a person feel best about themselves. They tell you in the tone of their speech, by their appearance and grooming, and by the people and things they surround themselves with. Think about it.*

---

*Love isn't something you can do to someone. It's something you let them feel about themselves by the message you give them that validates their own magnificence. Think about it.*

---

*If each person could honestly say, 'I like me best when I'm with me,' they would have the solution to all problems and the answer to all questions. Think about it.*

---

*There are four simple rules to follow that will allow folks to like themselves best when they're with you.*

*Rule #1: Let them know that anything they are embarrassed about or guilty about (especially from their past) is not their fault, and you're determined to prove it.*

*Rule #2: Never confront or attack anyone's sense of Guilt by 'should-ing' them.*

*Rule #3: Never infringe upon or override anyone's Agency or freedom of choice.*

*Rule #4: Find and point out every good quality that you see in others. Be completely blind to their weaknesses and faults. (And understand that disobeying this rule will guarantee your relationship a short life expectancy. This particularly applies to double-edged weapons such as 'constructive' criticism and direct accusation, because these are the very things that will punch them in the Agency and kick them in the Guilt.) Think about it.*

## 19

# The Four Confusions

*There is much concern in recent times regarding **enforcement** of laws. Throughout the history of mankind there has been much issue made of obedience to laws. (Obedience is actually the antithesis of the concept of Agency.) It is the contention of the Guardian force assigned to planet Earth and its human population that true understanding supersedes and obviates the need for the concepts of enforcement or obedience pertaining to the universal laws. If an individual truly understands a law, how it works, why it works, and the benefits of being in accord with the principle there would be true excitement to be in perfect alignment with that law. Think about it.*

---

*'Do unto others as you (I) would have them do unto you (Me.)' Golly gee, could this possibly be a concise version of the Law of Me? Think about it.*

---

*Here is a variation of the concept that is quite revealing of human nature. "The things I find objectionable in you I have in me, for if I did not have them in me I could not recognize them in you." It may be interesting to note that the great masters throughout history found very little objectionable in their fellow man, for they had long since lost those negative qualities in themselves. Think about it.*

---

*Who Am I? Am I who I think I am? Am I who you think I am? Or am I who I think you think I am?*
*Who am I? I am not who I think I am. I am not who you think I am. I am who I think you think I am.*
*Who Am I? I am who I am. I love whom I choose to be, therefore you can like you best when you're with me.*

*(A wise and wonderful woman who finished her life experience several decades ago, when faced with criticism or judgmentalism would simply respond by saying "Me am who me am." That simple comment alone summarized her own surety of the only approval she needed. Herself!) Think about it.*

---

*Faith is a most misunderstood concept. It is not dreaming, praying, and sitting around hoping in one hand and spitting in the other to see which gets full first. Faith is an ACTION word. The farmer may have faith that he will have a crop in the fall but he takes action to plow the field, plant the seed, weeds, nurtures and cultivates the crop, all the while praying for divine support. Then when the crop, whether great or small, has been harvested he takes possibly the most important action of all. He humbly expresses gratitude for the bounty he has received. Think about it.*

## 21

# A Return to Perfection

*The above concept does not allow license to repeat an action already proven to be inappropriate. It's Not Your Fault only applies if the outcome is not what, in retrospect, would have been intended.*

---

*Remember that anger and judgmentalism are the evil stepchildren of guilt. Guile is the vicious projection of anger and accusatory judgmentalism. Therefore a guileless person is devoid of the Guilt, which spawns guile. Think about it.*

---

*Jealousy is one of the greatest enemies of perfection. This applies to all elements of life: professional, personal, and intimate relationships such as marriage and divorce. Almost all jealous people conclude that any attraction their mate might have to someone else is a matter of their inadequacy when it may simply be a failure to understand the concept of "I like me best when I'm with you." So they almost always drive away the very person about whom they feel jealous or possessive. If they truly understood the concept they would always find ways to give their mates a chance to express themselves freely. So they would enhance the Agency of their significant other and not detract from it. Think about it.*

## 22

# Is The Pen Mightier Than the Sword?

*Will you understand and accept the fact that the past no longer exists? Or will you choose to recreate it by replaying the memory over and over again, beating yourself up and adjusting your memory downward—all over something that no longer exists? Think about it.*

## 23

# Justice Versus Just Is

*You can ensure "Justice" in your life by applying the law that "just is." Think about it.*

---

*The extent to which you are dependent is the extent to which you have given power over yourself to that upon which you depend. Every single fear known to man is prompted by a threat to some dependency. Independence, freedom and fearlessness result from taking control of the threat and its attending dependency. Think about it.*

---

*The majority of people, unfortunately, have gotten away from the tried and true financial principles of living within their incomes and saving a small portion no matter how meager their means. (There is also a universal law called The Law of the Tenfold Return [referred to as tithing in many spiritual belief systems] which would be worthy of investigation by anyone concerned with concepts of abundance and prosperity.) Think about it.*

---

*Being wise and well prepared can turn a disaster into an adventure. Think about it.*

---

*Very simply, with every debt, you literally give away a piece of your life. It would be wise to ask yourself, "Is that sound system, fancy car or too expensive home worth the chunk of my life I am trading for it?" Think about it.*

## 24

# The Law of Creation

*As you study the depths of creative philosophy within the major comprehensive belief systems of mankind you will discover a concept held in common between them. It is that "all things are created spiritually before they are create temporally." Think about it.*

---

*Maybe the counsel to 'become as little children,' when applying the necessary belief for creation is a valid perception that innocence of a negative history will spawn no doubt of a perfect outcome. Think about it.*

---

*There is a really simple trick to bypassing the un-creating, negative conscious thoughts and the reverse feelings that bubble up from the subconscious. When you set a goal or objective, visualize and think only of what you desire and why you want it. Never give any thought to how or whether you will obtain the objective. The universe is much more capable than you are of figuring out how to fill your needs. Don't fumble around and get in the way of your own creation because "How" thinking is a petri dish for growing the slime of doubt and depression, the great un-creators. Don't work so hard. Learn to sit back and enjoy the magnificence of your power to create. Think about it.*

---

*If every thought creates, it can be concluded that everyone creates and un-creates constantly. The difference between success and failure is the determination to simply create more than is uncreated. Think about it.*

---

*Fear of perfection, or our inability to achieve it, is one of the principal blocks to understanding the Law of Creation and applying it. People can't seem to get it that failure is just a stepping-stone to success. Many get so frozen with fear that they just don't try at all. The best remedy for that is just to do simple things first. Set small goals and objectives, and once you've mastered those, you can move on to something bigger and better. Remember one of the Four Agreements (by Don Miguel Ruiz) is: 'Just do your best.' The rest will follow.*

---

*Once you reach a certain level of understanding about the Law of Creation, you get to realize that every thought you have creates… something. So it's important to release all negativity and blockages in your life—every negative thought, every notion of rejection, failure and especially Guilt. One of the best ways to do that is through meditation. And three times daily is recommended. Most of us have about 18 waking hours in our average day. If you take about half an hour three times every day to get still, clear the clutter from your mind and get in touch with what Abraham Lincoln once called 'The Better Angels of our nature,' you'll be amazed at what you can actually create. Some people might call that making contact with the Holy Spirit. You may call it what you like. The secret lies in trusting the good forces in your life and allowing them to come in. And don't feel guilty about the feelings of joy and fulfillment you get when you do. Instead, start out with a profound sense of Gratitude for everything that you have. Life is a gift. Celebrate that gift. And don't forget to say "Thank you." Think about it.*

## 25

# Goals and Objectives: The Power of Faith

*A classic case of how Faith really works comes with the story of the man whose house is caught in a flood that virtually engulfs his entire home. Desperately, the man scrambles to his rooftop while the floodwaters come right up to the edge. Sitting on his roof peak, the man puts a prayer up to heaven. 'Dear Lord,' he prays.*

*'I place my faith in You. I know You will come and save me in my time of peril.' Convinced his prayers have been heard, the man waits for the miracle when a fellow comes along in a motorboat and offers to take him to safety. 'No, thanks,' the man on the roof says. 'I put my prayer to the Lord and He will save me.' So the motorboat motors away, and the man on the roof continues to wait.*

*A couple of hours later a large rescue barge comes along with hot food and Red Cross relief facilities and offers to take the man on the roof aboard. 'Oh no thanks,' the man tells the barge Captain. 'I put my prayer to the Lord and He will save me.' By now it's several hours later. The water continues rising, and the man is clinging to his chimney top when a helicopter comes overhead and drops down a ladder. 'Grab hold!' the helicopter pilot calls down to him. 'Oh, no thank you,' the man replies. 'I prayed to the Lord and I know the*

*Lord will save me.' Shortly thereafter the floodwaters rise over the man's whole house. He loses his grip and drowns. But since he's a decent man he goes to heaven. When he gets to the Pearly Gates, he expresses his disappointment to St. Peter that his prayers to God weren't answered, and that he was left to die. Surprised, St. Peter checks his log and says: 'I don't understand. It shows right here that we sent you two boats and a helicopter.' Think about it.*

———

*There is a very effective way to eliminate the unwanted in the image of creation. In other words, you can eliminate 'un-creation' before it has a chance to work its wicked little will on your game plan. And you can do that by the following: 1) Distracting–belief in something or someone outside yourself. 2) Psyching oneself up by joining the group dynamic, including prayer, meditation, rallies, meetings and chanting and other means of group expression. Most motivation 'gurus' use this means of meeting and pep-rally gathering to help get people focused. And this is especially effective in sports, using the team concept to get people motivated and focused on the game or event. 3) Eliminating flaws in the picture by releasing the anti-creation images in your success projection.*

*This third step involves something called The Steering Wheel Concept of management. It is very much like the way we drive our car to a destination. We know where we're going, and we know we'll get there. Still, we steer the wheel back and forth across the directional intention of our car through little acts of overcompensation, even as we're guiding our car toward our destination. We already have a perfect understanding of what we want to accomplish. We know we're going to get there. So we don't bother dealing with all the little reasons why it won't happen. Think about it.*

## 26

# Failure as the Pathway to Success

*People tend to learn very little or nothing from the easy times of their lives. Struggle, difficulty, and failure force people to do what they won't do when life is easy. The thing they won't do without being hit between the eyes with the proverbial "two-by-four" is to think and decide. If necessity is the mother of invention then terror is the father of pure inspiration. Think about it.*

---

*When you quit on life, trust me, life will quit on you. Think about it.*

---

*Failure often inspires the redirection from an incorrect path to the correct or intended goal. (The universe is always able to provide a better path to an objective than you can imagine on your own.) Think about it.*

---

*The most important step toward any objective is to decide. Everyone has heard the statement that 'leaders make decisions quickly and change them slowly and followers make decisions slowly and change them quickly.' Think about it.*

---

*Whatever your goal is, there are some inner qualities that lie within your power to help create the dynamics of success: 1) Decide. Most people fail because they fail to make a decision about what it is they truly want to do. Once you do decide, you'll sense a shift of energy in your favor that you can virtually feel. 2) Have a strong Desire to accomplish your objective. Your decision is only as effective as the mental, emotional and spiritual energy that fuels it. 3) Visualize. You should see yourself having accomplished your objective. Embrace all aspects of it. See it as already done. And do it at least twice every day. 4) Concentrate. All success is based upon the ability to focus one's energies magnificently. There's a universal law that says in effect: 'Whatever commands the majority of your attention expands.' If you focus and concentrate on the completion of your objective, success will be the result. 5) Willpower is often the difference between success and failure. Vince Lombardi once said: 'The difference between a successful person and others is not a lack of strength, not a lack of knowledge, but rather in a lack of will.'*

*People with true will power never quit, and because of that, they seldom fail. **6)** Usually will power is the twin of a quality called **Self-Discipline**. All the visualization and concentration in the world will accomplish nothing unless you discipline yourself to accomplish what you've set out to do. **7) Persist.** The greatest achievements in the world were often accomplished by people who others thought were too dumb to quit. President Calvin Coolidge once said: "Nothing in this world can take the place of persistence. Talent will not; nothing* *is more common than unsuccessful people with talent. Genius will not; unrewarded genius is almost a proverb. Education will not; the world is full of educated derelicts. Persistence and determination alone are omnipotent. The slogan "press-on" has solved and always will solve the problems of the human race."* Success always comes with a plan, failure with excuses. Think about it.

## 27

# Gratitude

*This little commentary on the electric fence issue has been stated in its shorter form from earlier in these discussions. Think about it, again.*

---

*The 'aha' of a truth, for which you are ready, will be so familiar, even though previously unknown, that it feels like a remembrance. Think about it.*

---

*That blissfully isolated individual we have just described would face each experience with the innocent, wide-eyed, childlike joy exemplified by the character of Jethro (of "The Beverly Hillbillies" fame) or Tarzan (of ape relations fame). Think about it.*

---

*Most successful people have been 'broke' (short on or without money) many times before they reach true success and prosperity. However, they never allow themselves to be 'poor' in the vision of how they see themselves. Think about it.*

---

*If folks put one half of the effort and creativity into the success and prosperity principles taught in and by thousands of self-help and success books, seminars, Scriptures, gurus, parents, Masters and summarized in these discussions I have brought you from the Guardian Council, that they put into cheating, stealing, conning, crime and unethical schemes, they would invariably be richer in a very short time than those from whom they steal. (It is truly a sorry commentary on the human race that some of the greatest minds can be found in prison.) Think about it.*

---

*History is replete with dictatorships and totalitarian governments being established by encouraging the resentment that "lack thinking" creates in the minds of the have-nots against the more intelligent and prosperous members of society. When the thinkers and the doers are eliminated, the poor unfortunate "lack thinking" are doomed to the true endless "lack" of servitude to the purest lack thinkers of all the political elite who produce nothing and steal everything. This is not intended as a political statement. We Guardians don't involve ourselves with such foolishness. This note is only intended to exemplify the terrible ultimate extreme of "lack thinking." Think about it.*

---

*What if one was to use the principle of gratitude in prayer? What if gratitude were expressed rather than a request made in prayer? Gratitude for a need having been filled (even before it has) is a considerably different creative state than praying and asking for the need to be filled. Think about it.*

---

*It is highly probable that if you think about it guilt is the result of ingratitude. (There are scriptures, which indicate that God considers ingratitude the greatest sin. The parents of many modern teenagers may have a strong tendency to agree.) Gratitude is an attitude—and the lack of gratitude is the greatest offense. Please understand: you can fix a mistake, but not an attitude. But interestingly enough, if you maintain the attitude of gratitude you will not make mistakes. Think about it.*

---

*Take each of the principles from the table of contents along with those from the various discussions and match them with Gratitude as an application. It's all about relationships. Look at the desert island concept. No relationships, no problems. The principle of Gratitude is most probably the solution to all human problems. This is pretty simple. But after all, shouldn't life be simple enough so that everyone can live it in peace, joy, happiness, love and abundance? If people didn't make life so hard and were simply grateful for who they are and the magnificence of all they can be they could joyfully achieve the full measure of their creation. Think about it.*

## ZONE A

# Baby, It's Not Your Fault!

*People can get pretty goofy sometimes when it comes to communication. Ask any blind person. They either get yelled at as if they're hearing impaired, or else others around them overcompensate for their blindness, and start to behave as if none of their other senses work either. Think about it.*

---

*There is an absolute law that states the following: "Whenever you see anger or judgmentalism you are always looking into the eyes of Guilt. (This is true even if the anger is **righteous indignation**. The Guilt is the result of frustration at the inability to fix the situation.) Think about it.*

---

*Then again, there is the young bachelor who falls into lust for a single mom who happens to have a very young child. She's got a kid, so he realizes that this is a package deal. Later, when they develop a relationship, he's watching NFL football on a Sunday night. The Redskins are making a goal line stand, and the game is on the line. With a sinister sense of perfect timing, the girlfriend's baby starts to cry. The boyfriend is done onto. The night is ruined. And 'the kid did it!' This begins a recipe for disaster. Think about it.*

## ZONE C

# It's Not Your Fault for Dogs

*In any animal/human relationship you have to ask yourself this question: Who is really the master here, and who has who trained? And how well are they trained? The dog goes to the door and barks once. The 'master' immediately gets up and goes over to open the door. So, when you really get down to it, we're observing 'one command' obedience here. How many folks have ever had a dog or a kid that was that well trained? Think about it.*

## ZONE D

# Addiction

*Forget heroin, cocaine, and marijuana. Most of the painkillers, stress-relief drugs and antidepressants are now sold by prescription in the billions of units. Brand name drugs such as Prozac, Zoloft, Paxil, Vicodin, and Lexapro are legal and yet can often become ticking time bombs. People who think they need them often get prescribed antidepressant cocktails that are variations of these formulations. And because they're issued under a doctor's car, people take them regularly by the billions of units a month. The result is that they have become victims in the Great American Prescription Drug Culture. In fact, once many patients get hooked on these antidepressant cocktails, their physicians literally cannot allow them to quit cold turkey because the two most frequent side effects of withdrawal are deep-depression and suicidal tendencies. Think about it.*

# What About You?

*If studying* THE GUARDIAN CODE: It's Not Your Fault [And I Can Prove It!] *has taught you anything it should be this: you have something of great value to bring to the world! That is why you were brought here. (You can and will make a difference, once you actually choose to do so.) And, since the secrets of this Code are hiding in plain sight, the best thing I can think of to tell you is…to look in the mirror! The thoughts you are thinking and the ideas you are formulating—especially since you just finished this journey with us—are most definitely worth their weight in gold. So recognize their value, write them down in front of you, and don't be shy about sharing them with the world. (Trust me, it would truly like to know) To help you, we're including a "Notes and Quotes" Section on the following pages…for you to use as your own book of wisdom—your observations and your plans for your life and your world. Think about it.*

*Have Faith, and remember that "faith" is an action word.*

— The Guardian.

## NOTES AND QUOTES

# NOTES AND QUOTES

## NOTES AND QUOTES

# NOTES AND QUOTES

## NOTES AND QUOTES

## NOTES AND QUOTES

# THE GUARDIAN CODE
## ESSENTIALS
### (ORDER TODAY!)

### THE GUARDIAN CODE
*It's Not Your Fault [And I Can Prove It!]*

This revolutionary book reveals the secrets to finding the magnificence in your life.

### MY BOOK OF LIFE
Begin with Gratitude, and take the Guardian Code's step-by-step program toward leading "the charmed life."

**Available in print from:**
**www.Amazon.com • www.BarnesAndNoble.com/ •**
**www.BooksAmillion.com**

**Available in electronic format from:**
**• Amazon Kindle • Nook •iBooks • Smashwords**